JUSTIN BIEBER

OUR WORLD

MILLIE ROWLANDS

INTRODUCING

Raw and pure talent is the only way to describe Justin Bieber. He sings, raps, break-dances, plays the guitar, piano, drums and the trumpet. And, of course, he's super cute!

What a whirlwind of a few years it's been for the guy. It was only a couple of years ago that the young prodigy was just a regular child with a passion for music. Now he's the most famous teenage musician on the planet. As they say, the guy's got it all. His voice and face is now known in every corner of the planet, and to think this is only the beginning…

JUSTIN!

BIEBER FEVER

'On my wall I have a picture of James Dean, a poster of Entourage, The Hangover poster, a picture of Tu Pac. I've also got a poster of a mouse with headphones on.'

A Star is Born!

A star was born on March 1st 1994 in the sleepy Canadian town of Stratford, Ontario. Baby Justin was a beautiful brown-eyed boy with a beaming smile that warmed the hearts of anyone that held him. However, Justin's early years were tough. His parents split up when he was very young. A troubling time for any kid: 'No kid likes to have their parents split up,' says Justin. 'You don't get to see them together but I got two Christmases, which is always a bonus… There's always ups and downs but mostly downs when it comes to parents splitting up. 'But, Justin has a mature attitude when it comes to talking about his parents and understands that his parents have always loved him very much, despite their own difficulties. 'When my parents split up and I helped my family get through it,' says Justin. 'I think a lot of kids have had their parents split up, and they should know that it wasn't because of something they did.'

BIEBER
FEVER

'I will never forget
where I once was –
and where I come
from.'

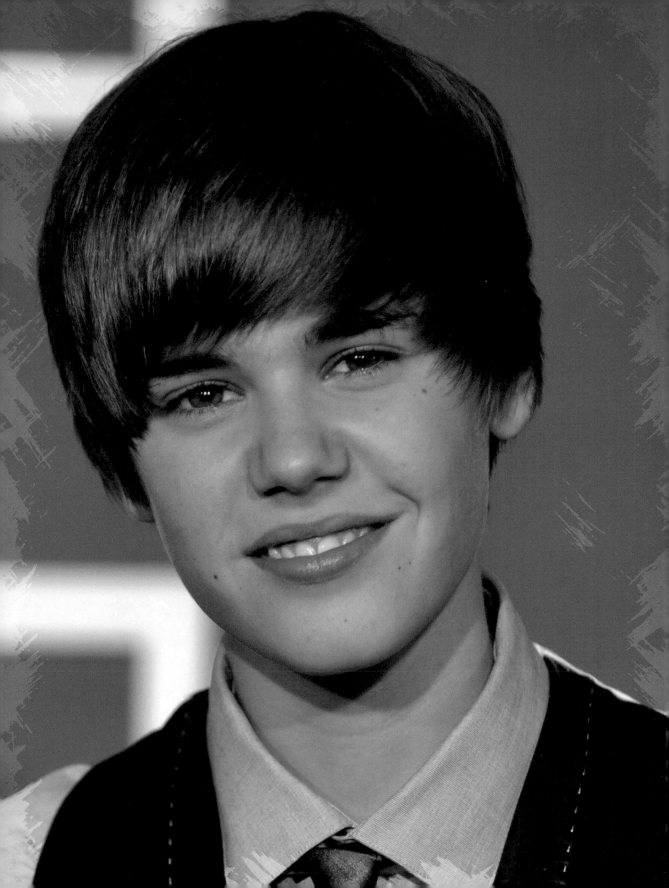

School Days

School wasn't much easier. It was difficult for his hardworking mother to raise enough money for her son to have all the fancy clothes some of the other kids could afford. Being raised by a single mother and living in public housing was very tough on the young boy. 'It was always hard but I definitely had a good life,' says Justin.

Some of the kids didn't like Justin and he got a hard time for being short and not having the coolest clothes. Thankfully Justin had an escape from all of his trouble in the form of music...and look where he is now! Not only is he an international superstar and heartthrob but he's down to earth too.

BIEBER FEVER

'I didn't have as much as other people did. I think it made me stronger as a person – it built my character.'

JUSTIN

Full Name: Justin Drew Bieber

Born: March 1st, 1994

Star Sign: Pisces

Height: 5'3½"

Siblings: Half-sister named Jazmine and a half-brother named Jackson

Pet: Dog called Sammy

Nicknames: J-Beebs, Beeb

Hometown: Stratford, Ontario, Canada

Current Home: Atlanta, Georgia

Car: A Range Rover bought for him by Usher for his 'Super Sweet 16'. Cool, huh?!

Record Label: Island Def Jam

Hero: Chuck Norris

Favourite sports: Ice hockey, soccer, baseball, skateboarding

Girlfriends: None

Celebrity Crush: Beyoncé

Favourite Colour: Blue

Favourite Food: Spaghetti and tacos

Favourite Cereal: Captain Crunch

Dislikes: Bling

Favourite Drink: Vitamin Water

Foreign Languages: French and he can count to ten in German!

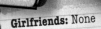

10

FACTBOOK

Phobia: Escalators and lifts — he suffers from claustrophobia

Favourite Pie: Apple pie

Favourite Candy: Sour Patch Kids

Favourite Colour To Wear: Purple

Favourite Sports Team: Toronto Maple Leafs

Best Friends: Ryan Butler, Christian Beadles and Chaz Somers

Favourite show: Smallville

Favourite Movie: Rocky

Favourite Saying: 'Single and Ready to Mingle'

He doesn't like chocolate (But loves Twix)

Party Trick: He can solve a rubik's cube in under a minute

Favourite Shoe Brand: Supra

Favourite Romantic Movie: *A Walk To Remember*

DISCOVERED!

Justin threw himself into music and chose to express himself that way. 'I started to play the drums at two years old, then I picked up the piano at eight, but I've never had a lesson.'

Justin started making money from his talents by busking in the streets. 'I used to play my guitar in my local city, so I would play outside and open up my guitar case, which people would throw any change into. I made $3,000 and took my mom on a vacation to Florida. That was pretty awesome.' Awww!

Justin's music became an obsession. He went on to master the drums, the trumpet, the guitar and the piano. Plus he can rap and break-dance!

On his iPod
Usher,
Ne-Yo,
Chris Brown,
2Pac,
Rascall Flatts,
Elliott Yamin,
Billy Talent,
Lifehouse,
and T-bone

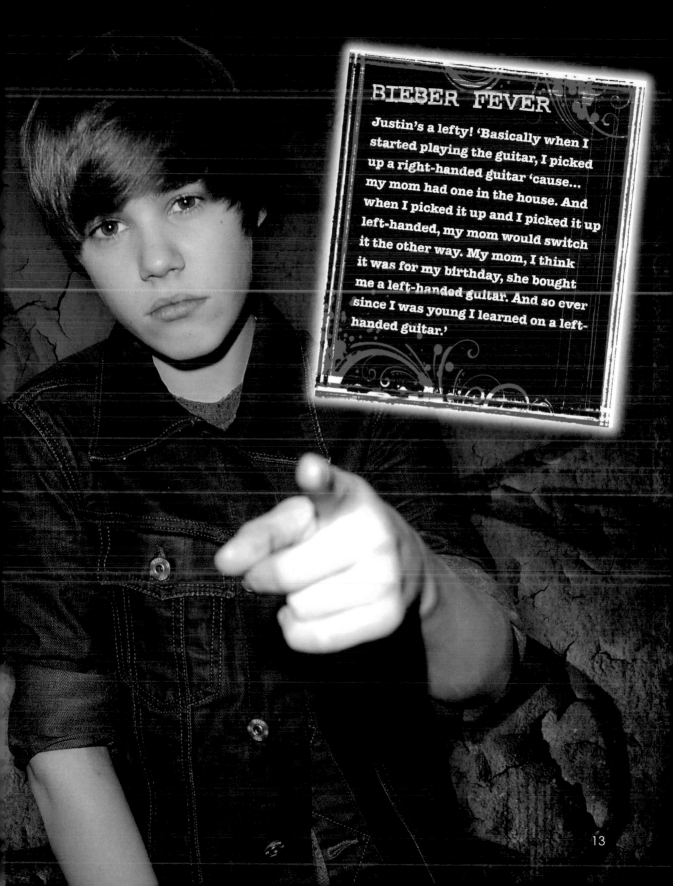

BIEBER FEVER

Justin's a lefty! 'Basically when I started playing the guitar, I picked up a right-handed guitar 'cause... my mom had one in the house. And when I picked it up and I picked it up left-handed, my mom would switch it the other way. My mom, I think it was for my birthday, she bought me a left-handed guitar. And so ever since I was young I learned on a left-handed guitar.'

13

BIEBER FEVER

Justin's YouTube account name is "kidrauhl"

Sing us a song, Justin!

Of all his talents, it was singing that truly launched Justin's career. Having honed his craft for a few years he decided to enter a local competition in his hometown. Justin came second, but sadly some of his friends and family couldn't make the live performance. Natalie, his mother, decided to post her son's performance on YouTube, a decision that would change their lives forever, and boy are we glad she did!

'I entered a local singing competition called Stratford Idol. The other people in the competition had been taking singing lessons and had vocal coaches. I wasn't taking it too seriously at the time, I would just sing around the house. I was only 12 and I got second place... my mom posted the video for other friends and family to see on YouTube and people seemed to really like it.'

14

Justin goes global

Encouraged by the popularity of his first vid, Justin began posting more videos of himself performing. His favourite covers at the time included songs by artists such as Usher, Ne-Yo and Stevie Wonder. Soon enough he started to build a lot of momentum and people all over the world were logging on to watch the latest teen sensation. Without any publicity or management Justin notched up 10 million views onto his YouTube account, purely by word of mouth! It really was that simple, says Justin: 'I put my singing videos from the competition on YouTube so that my friends and family could watch them. But it turned out that other people liked them and they started subscribing to them.'

BIEBER FEVER

For Stratford Idol, Justin performed Aretha Franklin's 'Respect', Matchbox 20's '3am', Alicia Keys's 'Fallin' and Ne-Yo's 'So Sick'.

15

In Demand

It wasn't long before the suits in the music biz started taking note of the online phenomenon and started promising Justin all sorts of deals and contracts. But Justin never dreamt that he could make it as a popstar by posting videos online. 'I was just posting videos online for fun. I never thought it (becoming a popstar) was possible. I never really dreamed of it.'

But soon the unthinkable was happening and the offers came thick and fast, says Justin: 'We were getting calls from lots of different managements and my mom didn't really know what was going on, or if it was real.'

The Call of Destiny

Just seven months after Justin started posting his videos online, former So So Def marketing executive Scooter Braun flew the then 13-year old singer to Atlanta to meet with his colleagues in the music business.

'Right when we flew into Atlanta, Scooter drove us to the studio and Usher was there in the parking lot, remembers Justin. 'That was my first time ever being out of Canada so I went up to him and was like, "Hey Usher, I love your songs, do you want me to sing you one?" He was like, "No little buddy, just come inside, it's cold out."'

BIEBER FEVER

According to JB his favourite part of meeting Justin Timberlake was meeting Timberlake's then girlfriend, Jessica Biel. 'That was the best part,' says Justin. 'She is so hot.'

The Fame Plane

Amazingly the first time Justin was ever on a plane was when he first flew to Atlanta on that trip with Scooter. 'First time I was ever on an airplane,' says Justin. 'It was amazing. ... I met Jermaine [Dupri, founder of So So Def], and then about a week later my manager had showed Usher the videos of me online.

'And Usher was like, "That was the kid? Man, that kid is ... I should have let him sing for me." And so, he flew me back to Atlanta where I got to sing for him and meet him. He then wanted to sign me. And then he got in contact with Justin Timberlake and JT also wanted to sign me.' Can you imagine?

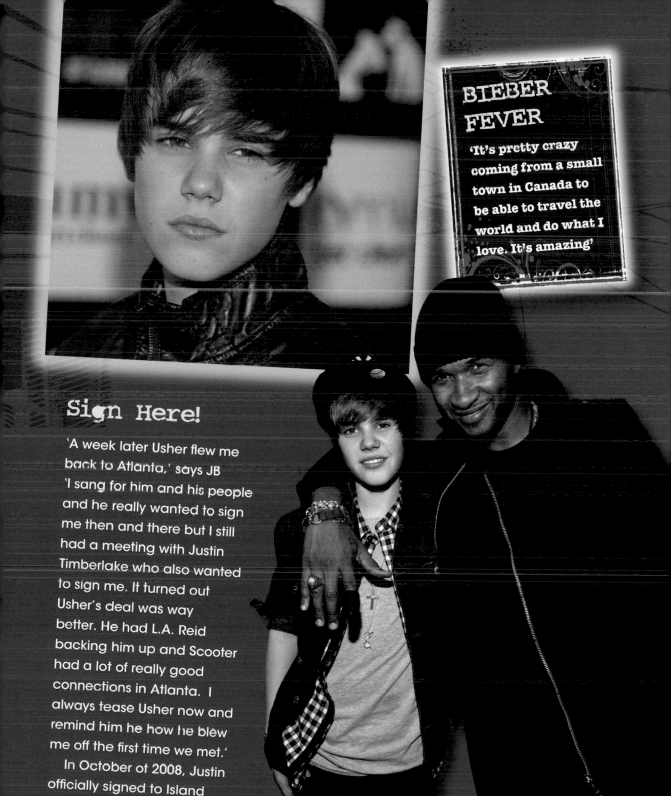

Sign Here!

'A week later Usher flew me
back to Atlanta,' says JB
'I sang for him and his people
and he really wanted to sign
me then and there but I still
had a meeting with Justin
Timberlake who also wanted
to sign me. It turned out
Usher's deal was way
better. He had L.A. Reid
backing him up and Scooter
had a lot of really good
connections in Atlanta. I
always tease Usher now and
remind him he how he blew
me off the first time we met.'
   In October of 2008, Justin
officially signed to Island
Records and Beiber Fever was set
to take over the world.

19

MAKING IT!

Getting discovered was only the beginning for Justin. The hard work was still ahead of him. Justin went straight into the studio and began recording his first single, 'One Time'. His debut single was written by Chris 'Tricky' Stewart and Terius 'The Dream' Nash. The two had also written Rhianna's 'Umbrella' and Beyoncé's 'Single Ladies', so Justin was in good hands. For Justin, recording his first track was an amazing experience plus he got to make the video in Usher's house. Quite a change from recording videos in his bedroom, says Justin: 'It was really cool going from my webcam to professional videos.'

BIEBER FEVER

Even after he's shot to stardom, Justin doesn't forget who his real friends are. The video for 'One Time' stars his best bud, Ryan. 'We've been best friends since we were little. We played hockey together and went to school together,' says Justin.

21

Platinum Baby!

Justin's first single, 'One Time', was released to radio while he was still recording his debut album. The song reached number 12 on the Canadian Hot 100 during its first week of release in July 2009 and later peaked at number 17 on the Billboard Hot 100. The song went Platinum in Canada and the U.S. and Gold in Australia and New Zealand. Justin was making his name around the world and he'd still only released just the one song. He set to work on his album, dreaming of further worldwide success.

BIEBER FEVER

'I love singing about love,' says Justin. 'That's what a lot of girls like listening to, and that's what I like to write.'

Justin's Party Playlist

'You Belong' — Taylor Swift

'Me and Taylor Swift have been dating for the past... no I'm just kidding,' says Justin! 'Taylor Swift and I have been twittering back and forth and she put her song and my video and I responded to her video. I actually met her the other day!'

'Mad' — Ne-Yo

'He is one of my favourite writers, he's awesome,' says Justin. 'Hopefully I'll get to work with him in the future.'

'Heartless' — Kanye West

'I did a cover of it on YouTube. Check it out on youtube.com/justinbieber.'

'Look So Good' — Jesse James

'Yes you do look so good... serious.'

'My Boo' — Usher

'Close friend, mentor and all that jazz.'

'Ego' — Beyoncé

'My future wife – just kidding! She's taken by Jay Z.'

'Sweet Dreams' — Beyoncé

'Yes she's in my sweet dreams.'

My World

The first half of Justin's two-part debut album, *My World*, was released on November 17th, 2009 and included the three hit singles 'One Less Lonely Girl', 'Love Me', and 'Favourite Girl'. As the title suggests, the album is all about Justin's world. 'It's a lot about love and teen love and what would be in my world.' But it's not just a soppy love-fest insists Justin: 'There's a lot of stuff there that's not just about love. There's songs that teens can relate to, as far as parents not being together and divorced. And just stuff that happens in everyday life… real life isn't perfect, so my album kind of portrays that. You just have to make the best of what you have.'

'Baby', the lead single from the second half of his debut album, My World 2.0, features Ludacris and was released in January 2010. The single became Justin's biggest hit to date, charting at number five in the U.S. and reaching the top ten in seven other countries. My World 2.0 also debuted at number one on the US, Canadian, Irish, Australian, New Zealand albums chart and reached the top ten in fifteen other countries.

THE FAME

In just over a year, Justin has gone from being a regular kid to the most famous teen on the planet. But how does he deal with all the attention? 'It's pretty hard to comprehend. Everything is, like, surreal. All my fans are really supportive, like on Twitter and everything. I'm just really glad that I get to do what I love.'

He has scores of people working for him and adoring fans who hang on his every word. But it's often hard to work out whom to trust and let into his crazy world. 'We're really sceptical on who we let into our team,' says Justin. 'We have a really small team. We really have fun. We've grown to be like a family. It's been incredible.'

GAME

BIEBER FEVER

What's the highlight of Justin's career so far? 'I got to perform for President Obama,' says Justin . 'That's probably at the top of things that I've done.'

Still Kidding Around

Justin is always aware of the fact that he has to remember to enjoy his childhood and not get too caught up in his hectic work filled world. 'We try and take out one day a week where I can go and be a regular kid. Just play basketball and go and hang out with my friends. Just do what I like to do. You know, sometimes for that day I just like to sleep, because the six days before that I've been exhausted.'

BIEBER FEVER

Did you know Justin is afraid of the dark? Awww!

BIEBER FEVER

Justin on nerves: 'I don't get nervous anymore because, you know, I do it so often but, like, I did when I first started.'

29

BIEBER FEVER

Justin's biggest fear? Being stuck in confined spaces. JB got stuck in an elevator when he was younger. And when he was seven, he played hide and seek with his cousin. His cousin shut him in a toy box and he got stuck in there. He's has been afraid of the dark and small spaces ever since.

Mum Knows Best!

Justin's a real mummy's boy and loves his mum more than anything in the world: 'She's a really strong woman,' says Justin 'She's been there since day one. She's just wanted me to be the best person that I could possibly be. She doesn't care about the money or the fame. She just wants to be my mom.'

He may be the most popular kid in the world but his mother still puts Justin in his place if he steps out line. If he is naughty or gets too big for his boots 'my mom usually takes away things that I really like, like my computer or my phone,' says Justin. 'I got my phone taken away for four days last week.'

And, of course, he still has a strict curfew that's carefully regulated by his mum. 'I have to be home by 10 o'clock and I usually get my computer taken away

BIEBER FEVER

The single 'One Time' isn't directed to a specific girl, it's directed at all girls.

from me by 10.30.' So it's not all fun fun fun, even if you are Justin Bieber!

But despite being very strict at times, Justin wouldn't swap having his mum with him for anything and loves having her on the road with him. 'It's great,' says Justin. 'She's a piece of home I get to take with me.'

The best advice Justin's mum has ever given to him? 'Stay humble.'

Justin insists all the attention hasn't affected him, and he's still a normal kid. 'I still feel regular,' he says. 'You know, sometimes it's weird that I go places and I have thousands of people waiting for me, but I always think, "I'm Justin".'

ON TOURBUS

Ever dreamed of going on tour with Justin?

Here's what we imagine it would be like...

Date: February 22nd

Location: Paris

Clothes: Red jacket, white T-shirt, blue jeans, black high-top trainers.

7am – Wake up, shower, style hair. 'First things first, every day, I've got to get ready for school,' says Justin.

8am – School with his personal tutor who travels with him wherever he goes. 'I go to school like everyone else. I do algebra, American history, English literature and biology. I don't really like biology,' says Justin. 'Today I'm learning about the Arc de Triomphe. When I travel I like to learn the history of each place that I go. Hopefully, you know, I'll get to go see it. Sometimes I don't get the chance cos I'm so busy doing work.'

10am – Press interviews. 'Today I have a really long day of press meetings ahead of me. Meeting people in the music business can get stressful sometimes. I always keep myself entertained.' Justin can speak some French so the language barriers in the interviews don't make things too difficult. 'I actually know some French. My grandparents' first language is French, so they taught me.'

12pm – Drive to private performance with mom. 'My mom travels with me everywhere we go... my mom keeps me level-headed.'

WITH JUSTIN

1pm – Private performance. 'I'm going to go and do a private performance so I'm really excited.' Justin plays for 30-odd adoring fans and plays hits such as 'Favourite Girl.' 'I love to go out there and play my guitar and sing for them and show them that I care about everything they've been doing for me.'

3pm – Unscheduled performance for fans in the street. 'The (private) performance was great, it was really intimate but I heard that there was hundreds of people outside that couldn't get in. So I decided to go to the window and play a little acoustic performance for them.' Always thinking of his fans, Justin plays for all his fans waiting for him in the cold Parisian streets. He performs songs such as 'Baby' for the hordes of cheering girls. 'That was like something out of the movies,' says his ever-humble mum.

5pm – Autograph signing for the masses of fans waiting for Justin outside the hotel. 'I couldn't just walk past them, I had to sign a few autographs.' Tough life, huh!

BIEBER FEVER

Justin always wanted to be a car mechanic when he was younger, so he was really happy with Usher's birthday present for his sweet 16. 'I got a Range Rover. It's my first car. I don't want to get too flashy,' says Justin. 'I always wanted to be a car mechanic.'

Date: February 23rd

Location: Paris

Clothes: Black leather jacket, black hat, black T-shirt, black jeans and silver chain.

8am – Radio interviews. 'Today I'm hitting up all the French radio stations about my upcoming album... Some of the French humour is a little crazy. They asked me some really weird questions and I'm only 15!'

2pm – Autograph signing at a mall. 'School was not in session so I heard that there were lots of people. It was so exciting just to meet all my French fans. I didn't know that a piece of paper with my name on it could mean so much to these kids.' Things get tough when the crowds and intensity make Justin feel sick. 'It was hot and crowded... I was overheated, I had to take a breather. I felt like I was going to throw up. My label people were like 'you're sick, you should stop'. I was like "No, I got to finish for these kids."'Justin endures feeling sick and continues signing autographs for his screaming and crying fans. 'It weird seeing girls cry. I'm honoured but why cry? You should be happy!'

5pm – Back to the hotel. 'I got to sleep!' says Justin.

BIEBER FEVER

So what does Justin get up to when he's not touring, doing interviews or in the studio? 'I like to do regular kids stuff. I like to play golf, I like to go to the movies with my friends. I like to shoot hoops,' says Justin. He's also a bit of an adrenalin junky and loves skateboarding. When he was in New Zealand he went bungee jumping! Most of all he loves hockey 'I love hockey,' says Justin . 'I played hockey all my life.'

Date: February 24th

Location: Paris

Clothes: Beige jacket, navy blue jeans, black T-shirt, blue baseball cap, blue high-top trainers.

10am – Sightseeing in Paris. 'Yesterday was a long day but I feel good today.' Justin gets to see the Arc de Triomphe that he learned about in class.

6pm – Autograph signing before a gig at the Eiffel Tower. Justin plays an acoustic set and does songs like 'Love Me' and 'Favourite Girl'. The crowd love it.

10pm. Home to catch up on Twitter and emails before going to bed.

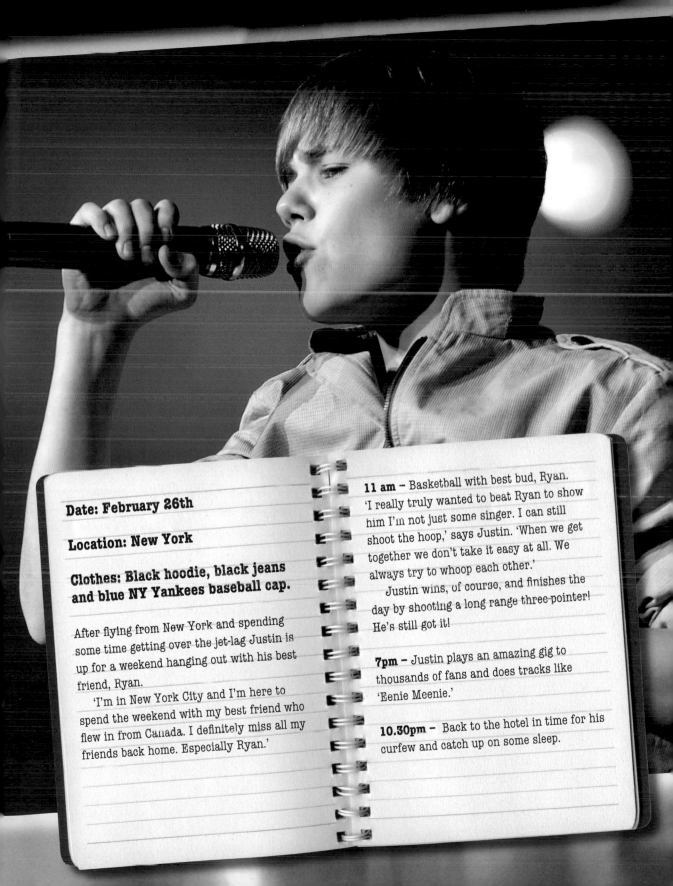

Date: February 26th

Location: New York

Clothes: Black hoodie, black jeans and blue NY Yankees baseball cap.

After flying from New York and spending some time getting over the jet-lag Justin is up for a weekend hanging out with his best friend, Ryan.

'I'm in New York City and I'm here to spend the weekend with my best friend who flew in from Canada. I definitely miss all my friends back home. Especially Ryan.'

11 am – Basketball with best bud, Ryan. 'I really truly wanted to beat Ryan to show him I'm not just some singer. I can still shoot the hoop,' says Justin. 'When we get together we don't take it easy at all. We always try to whoop each other.'

Justin wins, of course, and finishes the day by shooting a long range three-pointer! He's still got it!

7pm – Justin plays an amazing gig to thousands of fans and does tracks like 'Eenie Meenie.'

10.30pm – Back to the hotel in time for his curfew and catch up on some sleep.

JUSTIN'S CELEB

Now he's part of the A-list,

Justin gets to hang out with all the coolest peeps in Hollywood. But who's part of Justin's celebrity world?

Chuck Norris

Justin's biggest idol is the all-action hero, Chuck Norris. Justin loves him so much he even thanked Chuck in his album. As Justin says, 'Jesus can walk on water but Chuck Norris can swim through land.' Anyone who follows Justin on Twitter will see he continued messages of adoration he sends out about Chuck: 'Chuck Norris doesn't need Twitter,' jokes Justin. 'He's always following you.'

Beyoncé

Not only is she Justin's greatest celebrity crush, she's also one of Justin' favourite musical artists. 'Beyoncé, she's really hot. I just want to look at her. She's really talented, I'd like to work with her too.'

WORLD

Enrique Iglesias

Justin hopes to have as successful a career as the Latino heartthrob, who's a big fan of the little star. 'He's everywhere,' says Enrique of Justin. 'I've heard his music. I actually like that song he did with Ludacris, 'Baby'. It's hooky. It's a hooky song. I think he's a talented kid. It's so difficult to tell about the future. Judging by his talent, yeah, I think he has the ability. But will the kids be able to grow up with him as he moves on? It's all going to come down to the music he believes in. In this business, you're only as good as your last hit. As long as he keeps making really good hits, then yeah.'

Taylor Swift

Taylor and Justin have had a flirty friendship for a while with both of them dedicating songs to each other. Justin dedicated an online recording to Taylor. 'This song, 'Favourite Girl' is dedicated to you, Taylor Swift,' says Justin. 'This song is dedicated to you… because you are my favourite girl.'

Rihanna

Justin and Rihanna have some of the same songwriters, so they know each other's music very well. Of course, Rihanna's a huge fan! 'He has locked into an audience that have been missing someone for so long,' says Rihanna. 'They're going to grow with him because he seems very real - he's not forcing anything."

Usher

Usher is Justin's mentor. He knows better than anyone about Justin's amazing talent and could tell what huge potential he had as soon as Justin sang to him. 'Well, one was his voice, says Usher. 'I felt like his voice was incredible. I feel he was very charismatic, and that's what it takes to be able to handle what this is. It's the ability to turn it on and understand, but it was a very real ability. It was actually just him. If you ever met him, you'd understand exactly what I'm saying. The other side of it is just the fact that I felt like his story is yet to be told. I think we can go get him hit records or we can teach him how to dance or put him in front of some incredible lighting or put him in the right room and allow him to be himself. But also just his musical talent — the fact that he taught himself to play guitar, the fact that he taught himself to play piano to the point where he can write and create his own songs. [I said to him,] "You're a prodigy."'

BIEBER FEVER

Justin Bieber grew up listening to Boyz II Men. Justin said his mum played a lot of music around the house as he was growing up.

'She played a lot of R&B,' says Justin. 'Like Boyz II Men. That played in our house a lot. I would take the CD and take it in my room and try to do the little runs they did. And mimic what they were doing. ... Amazing.'

Snoop Dog

The veteran rapper was engaged in a chart battle with Justin Bieber when they both released albums at the same time. But Snoop doesn't hold any grudge against the young rival. 'I don't have no problem with that. That's what the music industry was made on,' says Snoop. 'I actually had a chance to meet the guy. He's kind of cool. So, I don't really have a problem with the teenyboppers or whatnot. Once upon a time, I was a young teenager coming into the game, driving 'em crazy and whatnot.'

Nicole Scherzinger

The Pussycat Doll and girlfriend of race driver, Lewis Hamilton has already had a flirtatious encounter with JB. 'He's a heartbreaker already,' says Nicole. 'Seriously, when I was recording "We Are the World," I was talking to Lionel Richie, Toni Braxton—there was a bunch of us in the room, and little Justin just walks in, he sits back, he puts his hand on his hips, and looks at me and goes, "I can't take it, I gotta leave. You're too gorgeous." And he walks out.'

Although Justin is 15 years younger than his crush, he still couldn't help but take notice. 'It was hard to take my eyes off her,' says Justin. 'She's so gorgeous!'

Ludacris

'Luda', as Justin calls him, featured on his track 'Baby'. The two are great pals with Justin learning plenty about the music biz from the older rapper. But according to Ludacris, young Justin doesn't need to know anything about women and, in fact, has taught Luda everything he knows about women! 'I get all my womanly advice from Justin,' says Ludacris. 'He's the one who tells me what I need to be doing.'

Justin agrees. 'I taught Ludacris everything he knows about girls,' says the young star.

DATING

Everything you need to know about Justin and dating

First kiss – age 13, at a school dance. He made the first move (song playing: 'How to Save A Life' by the Fray.)

Ideal girl – 'She has to be nice person and someone I can talk to,' says Justin. 'Because at the end of the day you can have the hottest girl in the world but if you can't sit there and have a conversation with her it's going to be terrible.'

Dislikes – 'I don't like girls who wear lots of make-up and you can't see their face,' says Justin. 'Some girls are beautiful but insecure and look much better without the make-up, but decide to put loads on.'

Justin is allowed to pick the girls for his videos – 'Yeah, they let me pick,' says Justin. 'I like a girl with a nice smile and eyes.'

Dating Justin – you'd have to impress his strict mother first. His mum said he couldn't date till he was 16. 'She did say that but she realised I was growing up, so now she doesn't mind,' says Justin. 'That was what she said to me when I was younger, but she knows that I date now.'

Most embarrassing moment – He was on a date with a girl at an Italian restaurant and he was wearing a white shirt. He ordered spaghetti and spilt it down the front of his shirt. They didn't go out again.

BIEBER FEVER

'James Dean is the inspiration for my look'

FACTFILE

Justin's Valentine – 'I have one person that I'll be sending flowers to and that's my mom. She's been there since the beginning and has given up a lot for me, I'm very blessed to have her. She likes roses.'

Justin on romance – 'I haven't been able to be as romantic as probably I will be able to be, but I think that being a gentleman is what matters; taking them out to a nice dinner, open the doors, stuff like that. Flowers are great, but love is better – you know what I mean?'

Justin's crushes – 'I have crushes, but they're all too old. Like Beyoncé – she has a husband, I might get shot. I went up to give Beyoncé a hug at the Grammys and Jay-Z said, "watch out buddy!" He was kidding, but you know...'

Would Justin ever consider dating a fan? 'It depends, it depends what the situation is. I think that I'm not going to limit myself.'

BIEBER FEVER

Justin has called Kim Kardashian his girlfriend before but he insists he was only kidding around and they're just friends. 'Kim Kardashian is a friend, a very sexy friend but a friend.'

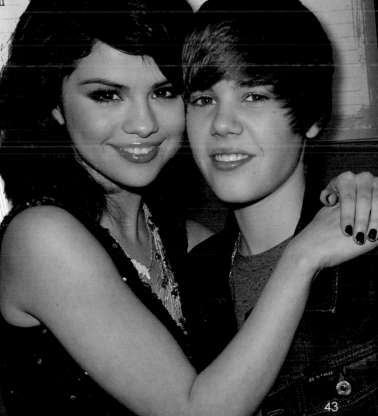

LOOKING TO

Growing up

JB's voice is now deeper than it was when he recorded his albums. The singer discussing his vocals says, 'It cracks. Like every teenage boy, I'm dealing with it and I have the best vocal coach in the world... Some of the notes I hit on 'Baby' I can't hit anymore. We have to lower the key when I sing live.'

As he gets older Justin understands that he's going to have to appeal to the older crowd as well as the kids. 'I think older people can appreciate my music because I really show my heart when I sing, and it's not corny, he says. 'I think I can grow as an artist and my fans will grow with me.'

THE FUTURE

What's next?

There's talk of more albums, collaborations and even movies in Justin's future. But looking ahead how does Justin see his career panning out? 'I'm looking forward to influencing others in a positive way,' says Justin. 'My message is you can do anything if you just put your mind to it. I grew up below the poverty line; I didn't have as much as other people did. I think it made me stronger as a person it built my character. Now I have a 4.0 grade point average and I want to go to college and just become a better person.'

45

PICTURE CREDITS
All pictures courtesy of Getty Images.
Background images: istockphoto

ACKNOWLEDGEMENTS
Orion would like to thank Guyan Mitra, Jane Sturrock,
Nicola Crossley, Helen Ewing, James Martindale, and Rich Carr

First published in hardback in Great Britain in 2010 by
Orion Books an imprint of the Orion Publishing Group Ltd
Orion House, 5 Upper St Martin's Lane, London WC2H 9EA
An Hachette UK Company

10 9 8 7 6 5

A CIP catalogue record for this book is available from the British Library.

ISBN: 978 1 4091 2315 6

Designed by www.carrstudio.co.uk
Printed in Canada

www.orionbooks.co.uk